Start Small, Dream Big:

A Beginner's Guide to Real Estate Investing with No Money Down

By

Madison Money

Table of contents

CHAPTER 1: INTRODUCTION

Investing in real estate is a great way to build wealth, but it can seem like a daunting task, especially if you don't have a lot of money to start with. The good news is, you don't need a lot of money to get started in real estate investing. With the right strategy, you can start small and still reach your big investment goals. This book, Start Small, Dream Big: A Beginner's Guide to Real Estate Investing with No Money Down, is your comprehensive guide to getting started in real estate investing, even if you don't have any money to invest.

In this book, you'll learn about the various strategies and techniques you can use to start investing in real estate with no money down. You'll discover how to find and evaluate properties, how to negotiate deals, and how to build a profitable investment portfolio, even if you're starting with a small budget. You'll also learn about the different types of real estate investments, such as rental properties, flipping, and wholesaling, and how to choose the right investment strategy for your goals and circumstances.

Whether you're a complete beginner or have some experience in real estate, Start Small, Dream Big will give you the tools you need to start building your wealth through real estate investing. With this book, you'll be able to overcome the financial barriers that often keep people from pursuing their investment dreams and start realizing your own real estate investment goals. So, if you're ready to take the first step towards financial freedom, grab a copy of Start Small, Dream Big today!

Why Real Estate Investing

Real estate investing has become a popular way for individuals to grow their wealth and build a passive income stream. There are several reasons why real estate investing is attractive:

Potential for High Returns: Real estate has the potential to provide high returns on investment, especially over the long term. This can be especially true in markets where property values are rising.

Inflation Hedge: Real estate is often considered a hedge against inflation, as property values can increase along with the cost of living.

Tangible Asset: Real estate is a tangible asset that you can see and touch, which can make it more appealing than investing in stocks or bonds.

Diversification: Real estate investments can help diversify an investment portfolio, reducing the overall risk of the portfolio.

Potential for Passive Income: Real estate investments, such as rental properties, have the potential to provide a passive income in the form of rental payments.

Tax Benefits: Real estate investing can also offer tax benefits, such as the ability to write off expenses related to the property, like mortgage interest and property management costs.

These are some of the reasons why real estate investing can be an attractive option for individuals looking to build wealth and create a passive income stream.

The Benefits of Starting Small and Dreaming Big

Starting small and dreaming big is a common strategy for those just starting out in real estate investing. There are several benefits to this approach:

Minimal Risk: By starting small, you can minimize your risk and test the waters before making a larger investment. This allows you to gain experience and learn about the market without risking a significant amount of money.

Affordability: Starting small also makes real estate investing more affordable, as you won't need to have a large amount of capital upfront to get started.

Flexibility: Starting with smaller investments allows you to be more flexible and pivot quickly if needed. You can also learn from your mistakes and make adjustments to your strategy without losing a significant amount of money.

Ability to Scale: Once you've had success with small investments, you can then scale up and invest in larger properties, thereby growing your portfolio and increasing your income potential.

Better Understanding of the Market: Starting small gives you a chance to gain a better understanding of the real estate market and how it operates, which can be especially valuable for beginners.

Dreaming big, on the other hand, provides motivation and a long-term vision for your real estate investing journey. It helps you stay focused on your goals and work towards creating the financial freedom and security you desire.

By combining the benefits of starting small and dreaming big, you can build a solid foundation for your real estate investing journey and achieve your long-term financial goals.

What You Will Learn in This Guide

In this guide, "Start Small, Dream Big: A Beginner's Guide to Real Estate Investing with No Money Down," you will learn:

The basics of real estate investing: You'll gain an understanding of what real estate investing is, different types of real estate investments, and the factors to consider before investing.

No money down strategies: You'll learn about various strategies for investing in real estate with no money down, such as owner financing, lease options, house hacking, partnerships, and government grants.

How to find the right property: You'll learn about the importance of location, conducting market research, analyzing the property's potential, and building your team of advisors.

Negotiating the deal: You'll learn how to understand the seller's motivations, make an offer, and close the deal.

Managing and growing your investment: You'll learn how to effectively manage your property, improve it for increased income, and find new investment opportunities.

By the end of this guide, you will have a good understanding of how to start small and dream big in real estate investing, and you'll be equipped with the knowledge and skills you need to successfully invest in real estate with no money down.

CHAPTER 2: UNDERSTANDING REAL ESTATE INVESTING

Types of Real Estate Investments

There are several types of real estate investments, each with its own unique characteristics and benefits. Some of the most common types of real estate investments include:

Residential properties: This type of real estate investment involves the purchase of single-family homes, multi-family dwellings, or vacation properties for the purpose of generating rental income.

Commercial properties: This type of real estate investment involves the purchase of commercial buildings such as office buildings, retail spaces, or industrial buildings for the purpose of generating rental income.

Raw land: This type of real estate investment involves the purchase of undeveloped land with the intention of holding it for future development or sale.

REITs (Real Estate Investment Trusts): This type of real estate investment involves investing in a trust that owns and manages a portfolio of properties. REITs provide investors with access to a diverse range of properties and the opportunity to invest in real estate without the hassle of direct property ownership.

Development projects: This type of real estate investment involves financing the construction or rehabilitation of properties with the intention of selling them for a profit.

Real estate crowdfunding: This type of real estate investment allows individuals to pool their money to invest in real estate projects, providing access to larger and more diverse real estate investments.

Each type of real estate investment has its own unique risks and rewards, and it's important to carefully consider the investment strategy that's right for you before making a commitment. This guide will help you understand the different types of real estate investments and how to make informed investment decisions.

Factors to Consider Before Investing

Before investing in real estate, there are several important factors to consider. These include:

Location: The location of the property is one of the most important factors to consider when investing in real estate. Properties in desirable locations with strong job markets, good schools, and low crime rates tend to appreciate value over time and attract reliable tenants.

Market conditions: It's important to have a good understanding of the current real estate market, including supply and demand, rental rates, and trends in property values.

Property condition: The condition of the property will have a major impact on its rental potential and resale value. It's important to thoroughly inspect a property before making an investment to ensure that it is in good condition and doesn't have any major repairs or renovations that need to be made.

Investment goals: It's important to have clear and realistic investment goals, such as generating passive income, wealth creation, or tax benefits. This will help you make informed investment decisions and stay focused on your goals.

Risk tolerance: Real estate investing carries risks, and it's important to have a good understanding of your risk tolerance before making an investment. Some investments, such as development projects, carry higher risks than others, such as REITs.

Financing options: Financing options, such as loans and mortgages, can greatly impact the return on your investment. It's important to understand your financing options and the terms and conditions associated with each.

By carefully considering these factors before investing in real estate, you can make informed investment decisions and increase your chances of success.

The Risks and Rewards of Real Estate Investing

Like any investment, real estate investing involves both risks and rewards. Some of the potential risks associated with real estate investing include:

Market risk: Real estate values can be affected by changes in the housing market, such as interest rate changes, economic downturns, and changes in local zoning laws.

Tenant risk: The rental income generated by a property is dependent on finding and retaining tenants. Tenant risk can be mitigated by conducting thorough background checks and screening tenants, as well as maintaining the property in good condition.

Maintenance and repair costs: Property ownership comes with the responsibility of maintaining and repairing the property. This can be costly, especially if major repairs are needed.

Financing risk: Financing options, such as loans and mortgages, can greatly impact the return on your investment. It's important to understand the terms and conditions associated with each financing option and the risks associated with borrowing money.

Despite these risks, real estate investing can offer a range of rewards, including:

Potential for passive income: Real estate investing can provide a steady stream of rental income, which can be a valuable source of passive income.

Appreciation: Over time, well-selected real estate investments can appreciate in value, providing a source of wealth creation.

Tax benefits: Real estate investing can offer significant tax benefits, such as deductions for mortgage interest and depreciation.

Control and flexibility: Unlike many other investments, real estate investing provides a high degree of control and flexibility, allowing investors to make decisions about how their investment is managed and how it is used.

By carefully considering the risks and rewards associated with real estate investing, you can make informed investment decisions and maximize your potential for success.

CHAPTER 3: NO MONEY DOWN STRATEGY

Owner Financing

Owner financing is a type of financing that allows a property owner to finance the purchase of their property rather than a traditional lender, such as a bank. In an owner financing arrangement, the property owner acts as the lender and provides the buyer with a loan to purchase the property. The loan is typically paid back over time, with interest.

Some of the benefits of owner financing include:
No need for traditional financing: Owner financing can be a good option for buyers who cannot secure traditional financing from a bank or other lender.

Flexibility: Owner financing arrangements can be more flexible than traditional financing, as the terms and conditions of the loan can be negotiated directly between the buyer and the seller.

Potential for a better deal: Owner financing can provide buyers with a better deal, as the interest rate and repayment terms can be more favorable than traditional financing.

However, owner financing also involves risks and considerations, including:

Default risk: The buyer may default on the loan, which could result in the loss of the property and the funds invested in it.

Legal considerations: Owner financing arrangements can be complex and should be carefully documented to ensure compliance with state and federal laws.

Interest rate risk: The buyer may be paying a higher interest rate than they would with traditional financing, which could increase the cost of the loan.

It's important to carefully consider the terms and conditions of an owner financing arrangement, as well as the potential risks and rewards, before entering into such an arrangement. In addition, it's recommended to seek the guidance of a qualified legal professional to ensure compliance with all applicable laws and regulations.

Lease Options

A lease option is a type of agreement that allows a tenant to rent a property with the option to purchase the property in the future. In a lease option, the tenant-buyer pays a portion of the rental payment towards the purchase price, and this amount is credited towards the purchase price if the tenant-buyer decides to exercise the option to purchase.

Some of the benefits of lease options include:

Ability to build equity: The tenant-buyer can build equity in the property over time through their rental payments, which can be credited towards the purchase price if they decide to exercise the option to purchase.

Flexibility: Lease options provide the tenant-buyer with the flexibility to decide whether or not they want to purchase the property in the future, without being obligated to do so.

Option to lock in a purchase price: The tenant-buyer can lock in the purchase price of the property at the time the lease option is entered into, which can protect them from price increases in the future.

However, lease options also involve risks and considerations, including:

Default risk: The tenant-buyer may default on the rental payments, which could result in the loss of the option to purchase the property and the funds invested in it.

Legal considerations: Lease options can be complex and should be carefully documented to ensure compliance with state and federal laws.

Option fee risk: The tenant-buyer may pay an option fee for the right to purchase the property, which may not be refundable if they choose not to exercise the option.

It's important to carefully consider the terms and conditions of a lease option, as well as the potential risks and rewards, before entering into such an arrangement. In addition, it's recommended to seek the guidance of a qualified legal professional to ensure compliance with all applicable laws and regulations.

House Hacking

House hacking is a strategy that allows an individual to purchase a multi-unit property and live in one unit while renting out the others. The rental income from the other units can help offset the cost of the mortgage, taxes, insurance, and other expenses associated with owning a property.

Some of the benefits of house hacking include:

Reduced housing costs: By living in one unit and renting out the others, the homeowner can significantly reduce the cost of housing.

Potential for positive cash flow: If the rental income from the other units exceeds the expenses associated with owning the property, the homeowner may enjoy the positive cash flow.

Potential for appreciation: Real estate has historically appreciated over time, and owning a multi-unit property can provide the homeowner with exposure to this potential appreciation.

However, house hacking also involves risks and considerations, including:

Management responsibilities: The homeowner is responsible for managing the rental units, which can be time-consuming and challenging.

Maintenance and repair costs: The homeowner is responsible for maintaining and repairing the property, which can be expensive.

Tenant-related risks: The homeowner may face challenges with tenants, such as late rent payments, property damage, or evictions.

It's important to carefully consider the costs, responsibilities, and potential risks and rewards of house hacking before entering into such an arrangement. In addition, it's recommended to seek the guidance of a real estate professional to ensure a successful experience.

Partnerships and Joint Ventures

Partnerships and joint ventures are arrangements in which two or more individuals come together to invest in real estate. In a partnership, the partners typically share in the profits and losses of the investment, while in a joint venture, the partners may have a more limited relationship and may not share in the profits and losses of the investment in the same manner.

Some of the benefits of partnerships and joint ventures include:

Pooled resources: Partners can pool their resources, including their money, time, and expertise, to invest in real estate that they may not have been able to afford or manage on their own.

Shared responsibilities: Partners can share the responsibilities associated with owning and managing real estate, which can reduce the workload for each individual.

Diversification: Partners can invest in different properties or markets, which can provide them with exposure to different types of real estate and help diversify their portfolios.

However, partnerships and joint ventures also involve risks and considerations, including:

Differing goals and objectives: Partners may have different goals and objectives for the investment, which can lead to disagreements and conflicts.

Legal considerations: Partnerships and joint ventures should be carefully documented to ensure compliance with state and federal laws and to avoid misunderstandings and disputes.

Sharing profits and losses: Partners are typically required to share in the profits and losses of the investment, which can be challenging if the investment is not successful.

It's important to carefully consider the terms and conditions of a partnership or joint venture, as well as the potential risks and rewards, before entering into such an arrangement. In addition, it's recommended to seek the guidance of a qualified legal professional to ensure compliance with all applicable laws and regulations.

Government Grants and Programs

There are several government grants and programs available for individuals looking to invest in real estate. These programs can provide financial assistance for things such as down payments, closing costs, and rehabilitation or renovation expenses.

Some of the most popular government grants and programs for real estate investors include:

Federal Housing Administration (FHA) loans: FHA loans are government-insured loans that offer low down payment options and flexible credit requirements. They are a popular option for first-time homebuyers and those with limited funds for a down payment.

Veterans Affairs (VA) loans: VA loans are government-backed loans specifically for military veterans, service members, and surviving spouses. They offer zero down payment options and relaxed credit requirements.

USDA Rural Development loans: USDA Rural Development loans are government-insured loans for individuals looking to purchase a home in a rural area. They offer low down payment options and flexible credit requirements.

State and local housing agencies: Many state and local housing agencies offer grants and programs for individuals looking to purchase or improve their homes, including down payment assistance, rehabilitation grants, and tax credits.

It's important to note that these programs may have specific eligibility requirements and restrictions, and that funding for these programs may be limited. It's recommended to research the specific requirements and restrictions of these programs and to seek the guidance of a financial professional to determine which program may be the best fit for your needs.

CHAPTER 4: FINDING THE RIGHT PROPERTY

The Importance of Location

The location of a real estate property is one of the most important factors to consider when investing. Location can impact a property's value, rental income, and potential for appreciation.

Some of the key factors to consider when evaluating a location include:

Demographics: The population, age, income, and education level of residents in the area can provide insight into the potential demand for rental properties and the stability of the local housing market.

Economic conditions: The local economy, employment opportunities, and the overall health of the housing market can impact the demand for rental properties and the potential for appreciation.

Proximity to amenities: Properties that are located near shopping centers, schools, parks, and other amenities are often in high demand and can command higher rents.

Transportation: Properties located near major transportation hubs, such as highways and public transportation, can be more convenient for tenants and may be in higher demand.

Crime rate: Properties located in areas with high crime rates may be more difficult to rent and may pose a higher risk for the investor.

It's important to thoroughly research the location of a property before investing, as the location can have a significant impact on the potential for the success of the investment. In addition, it's recommended to seek the guidance of a real estate professional with expertise in the local market to gain a deeper understanding of the location and its potential.

Conducting Market Research

Conducting market research is an important step in the process of real estate investing. Market research helps investors gain a better understanding of the local housing market, the demand for rental properties, and the potential for appreciation.

Some of the key aspects of conducting market research include:

Evaluating rental demand: Research the local rental market to determine the demand for rental properties and the average rental rates in the area.

Assessing the local housing market: Analyze the local housing market to determine the average home prices, the rate of appreciation, and the stability of the market.

Studying the local economy: Research the local economy to determine the health of the housing market and the potential for future growth.

Conducting a competitive analysis: Study the properties and landlords in the area to determine the competition and the potential for success.

Researching government regulations and zoning laws: Familiarize yourself with the government regulations and zoning laws in the area, as they can impact the potential for the success of the investment.

Conducting market research can provide valuable insights into the local housing market and can help investors make informed decisions about their investments. It's recommended to seek the guidance of a real estate professional with expertise in the local market to gain a deeper understanding of the market and its potential.

Analyzing the Property's Potential

Analyzing the potential of a real estate property is a crucial step in the process of real estate investing. This analysis helps investors determine the potential for rental income, the potential for appreciation, and the potential risks and expenses associated with the property.

Some of the key aspects of analyzing a property's potential include:

Evaluating the property's condition: Assess the physical condition of the property, including the condition of the roof, electrical and plumbing systems, and other major systems and components.

Determining the property's rent potential: Research the local rental market to determine the average rental rates for properties similar to the one being considered and determine the potential rental income for the property.

Projecting expenses: Estimate the costs associated with owning and maintaining the property, including mortgage payments, property taxes, insurance, and ongoing maintenance and repair costs.

Evaluating the property's appreciation potential: Analyze the local housing market to determine the potential for appreciation, as well as the factors that may impact the property's value over time.

Conducting a market and financial analysis: Evaluate the market conditions and the financial projections for the property to determine the potential for success and the risk involved in the investment.

Analyzing a property's potential can provide valuable insights into the potential for success and the risks involved in a real estate investment. It's recommended to seek the guidance of a real estate professional or financial advisor to gain a more thorough understanding of the property and its potential.

Building Your Team of Advisors

Building a team of advisors is an important step in the process of real estate investing, as it can provide valuable support and guidance throughout the investment process. A strong team of advisors can help investors make informed decisions, minimize risk, and maximize the potential for success.

Some of the key members of a real estate investment team include:

Real estate agent: A real estate agent can provide valuable insights into the local housing market, assist with finding properties, and negotiate on behalf of the investor.

Real estate attorney: A real estate attorney can provide legal guidance on real estate transactions, contracts, and other legal matters.

Accountant: An accountant can provide financial advice, help manage finances and tax implications, and provide guidance on investment strategies.

Home inspector: A home inspector can provide a comprehensive evaluation of the property's physical condition and identify any potential issues or repairs.

Property manager: A property manager can assist with the day-to-day operations of the investment property, including finding and managing tenants, handling maintenance and repairs, and collecting rent.

Building a strong team of advisors is an important step in the process of real estate investing, as it can help ensure the success of the investment and minimize risk. It's recommended to seek out advisors who have experience and expertise in the local housing market and in the specific type of real estate investment being considered.

CHAPTER 5: NEGOTIATING THE DEAL

Understanding the Seller's Motivations

Understanding the motivations of the seller is an important part of negotiating a successful real estate deal. Some of the common motivations for sellers include:

Time constraint: The seller may need to sell the property quickly due to time constraints, such as a job relocation or financial hardship.

Liquidity: The seller may need to sell the property to access the equity they have built up in the property and turn it into liquid assets.

Health issues: The seller may need to sell the property due to health issues or a change in their living situation.

Investment opportunities: The seller may have found another investment opportunity and needs to sell the property to free up capital.

Divorce or separation: The seller may need to sell the property as part of a divorce or separation settlement.

Retirement: The seller may want to downsize or sell the property as part of their retirement plans.

It is important to understand the seller's motivations so that you can tailor your negotiation strategy accordingly. For example, if the seller is under time pressure to sell, you may be able to negotiate a better price by offering a quick closing. On the other hand, if the seller is looking to maximize the sale price, you may need to make a higher offer or find creative financing solutions to close the deal.

By understanding the seller's motivations, you can also identify their pain points and find ways to address them during the negotiation process. For example, if the seller is under a time constraint, you can offer a quick closing or help them with moving expenses. If the seller is looking to maximize their return on investment, you can offer a higher price or find creative financing solutions that work for both parties.

In addition to understanding the seller's motivations, it is also important to be aware of the market conditions and understand the property's value. This will help you make informed offers and negotiate effectively with the seller.

By taking the time to understand the seller's motivations and market conditions, you can increase your chances of negotiating a successful real estate deal that meets your goals and the seller's needs.

Making an Offer

Making an offer is an important step in the real estate investing process. Here are some key considerations when making an offer:

Determine the property's value: Before making an offer, it is important to determine the property's market value. This will help you make a realistic offer and avoid overpaying for the property. You can use online tools, such as Zillow, or hire a professional appraiser to determine the property's value.

Consider your financing options: Before making an offer, it is important to consider your financing options. For example, if you are using a mortgage to finance the property, you will need to get pre-approved for a loan and determine the maximum amount you can afford to offer.

Take into account the seller's motivations: As discussed earlier, it is important to understand the seller's motivations so that you can make an offer that meets their needs. For example, if the seller is under a time constraint, you can offer a quick closing to increase your chances of getting the property.

Make a competitive offer: When making an offer, it is important to make a competitive offer that takes into account the property's market value and the seller's motivations. You can use the property's market value as a starting point and adjust your offer based on your analysis of the property and the seller's motivations.

Be prepared to negotiate: Real estate negotiations are often a back-and-forth process, and it is important to be prepared to negotiate with the seller. Be flexible, listen to the seller's needs, and be open to making compromises to close the deal.

Include contingencies: Contingencies are conditions that must be met before the deal can close. Common contingencies include a home inspection contingency, a financing contingency, and an appraisal contingency. By including contingencies in your offer, you can protect yourself from potential risks and ensure that the deal is in your best interest.

Consider the terms of the offer: When making an offer, it is important to consider the terms of the offer, such as the closing date, the deposit amount, and any contingencies. Make sure that the terms of the offer are favorable to you and aligned with your goals.

Have all necessary documents ready: When making an offer, it is important to have all necessary documents ready, such as a pre-approval letter, proof of funds, and a purchase agreement. Having these documents ready will make the negotiation process smoother and increase your chances of closing the deal.

Work with a real estate agent: If you are new to real estate investing, it is advisable to work with a real estate agent who can help guide you through the process of making an offer. A real estate agent can provide valuable insights, advice, and support, and help you negotiate with the seller.

By following these tips, you can increase your chances of making a successful offer and closing the real estate deal. It is important to remember that the real estate market is constantly changing, and it is essential to stay informed and adapt to changes in market conditions.

Closing the Deal

Closing the deal is the final step in the real estate investing process and requires careful planning and preparation. Here are some key considerations when closing a real estate deal:

Review the purchase agreement: Before closing the deal, it is important to review the purchase agreement to make sure that all terms and conditions are in order. Make sure that the purchase agreement accurately reflects the terms of the offer and any negotiated changes.

Coordinate with all parties involved: Closing a real estate deal involves coordination with various parties, including the seller, the buyer, the real estate agent, and the lender. It is important to communicate with all parties involved to ensure that everyone is on the same page and that the closing process runs smoothly.

Obtain title insurance: Title insurance protects you against title defects, such as liens or encumbrances on the property. Before closing the deal, it is important to obtain title insurance to protect your investment.

Close the deal at a title company: Most real estate deals are closed at a title company, where the transfer of ownership is completed and all necessary documents are signed. A title company can also assist with obtaining title insurance and handling other details related to closing the deal.

Prepare for closing costs: Closing costs are fees associated with closing a real estate deal and can include title insurance, appraisal fees, and closing fees. It is important to prepare for these costs and to have a clear understanding of all expenses involved in closing the deal.

Final walk-through: Before closing the deal, it is advisable to conduct a final walk-through of the property to ensure that any agreed-upon repairs have been made and that the property is in the same condition as when you made the offer.

Review closing documents: Before closing the deal, it is important to review all closing documents to make sure that everything is in order and that all terms and conditions are accurate.

Transfer funds: At closing, you will need to transfer the funds for the purchase of the property. This can be done through a wire transfer, cashier's check, or other means, depending on the agreement with the seller and the title company.

Record the deed: After closing the deal, the deed to the property should be recorded with the local government. This is an important step in ensuring that the transfer of ownership is legally recognized and that you have a clear title to the property.

By following these tips, you can ensure that the closing process is seamless and that you are fully prepared for the transfer of ownership. It is important to remember that closing a real estate deal is a significant investment and requires careful planning and preparation to ensure a successful outcome.

Managing and Growing Your Investment

Property management is the process of overseeing and maintaining a rental property, including managing tenants, collecting rent, and handling maintenance and repair issues. Here are some key considerations for property management:

Screen tenants: Screening tenants is an important step in property management, as it helps to ensure that you have responsible and reliable tenants who will take care of your property. This process typically includes conducting a background check, credit check, and verification of employment and rental history.

Set rent prices: Setting the right rent price is crucial for property management, as it will determine the return on your investment. It is important to research the local rental market to determine a fair and competitive rental price for your property.

Maintain the property: Maintaining the property is an important aspect of property management, as it will keep the property in good condition and attract high-quality tenants. This includes regular maintenance and repairs, as well as addressing any health and safety issues.

Collect rent: Collecting rent is an important part of property management, as it ensures that you receive a steady income from your rental property. It is important to establish a rent collection process that is efficient, reliable, and in compliance with local laws and regulations.

Handle tenant issues: As a property manager, you will need to handle various tenant issues, such as maintenance requests, lease violations, and disputes. It is important to have a process in place for addressing these issues in a prompt and professional manner.

Legal compliance: Property management also involves ensuring that your rental property is in compliance with local, state, and federal laws and regulations. This includes adhering to fair housing laws, health and safety regulations, and property tax requirements.

Marketing and advertising: Marketing and advertising your rental property is an important part of property management, as it helps to attract high-quality tenants and fill vacancies quickly. This may include listing the property on popular rental websites, hosting open houses, and utilizing social media and other marketing channels.

Record-keeping: Keeping accurate records is a crucial aspect of property management, as it helps to ensure that you have a clear and detailed record of all transactions, expenses, and income from your rental property. This includes keeping records of rent payments, maintenance expenses, and other relevant financial transactions.

Regular property inspections: Regular property inspections are an important part of property management, as they help to ensure that the property is well-maintained and in good condition. During these inspections, you can assess the property, address any maintenance or repair issues, and ensure that your tenants are following the terms of the lease agreement.

By following these tips, you can ensure that your property management process is efficient, effective, and in compliance with all relevant laws and regulations. It is important to remember that property management is an ongoing process and requires dedication and attention to detail to ensure success.

Property Management

Improving the Property for Increased Income

Improving the property is a key strategy for increasing income from a rental property. Here are some ways to improve a property and increase rental income:

Renovate and upgrade: Renovating and upgrading the property can significantly improve its value and attract higher-paying tenants. This may include updating the kitchen and bathrooms, adding new flooring, and making other cosmetic improvements.

Increase energy efficiency: Making energy-efficient upgrades, such as installing energy-saving appliances, new windows, and insulation, can reduce the property's operating costs and increase its value.

Add amenities: Adding amenities, such as a pool, fitness center, or community room, can increase the property's value and attract higher-paying tenants.

Maximize rental space: Maximizing rental space by adding additional units, such as a basement or attic conversion, can increase the property's income potential.

Implement a strong marketing strategy: Implementing a strong marketing strategy can help to attract high-quality tenants and increase rental income. This may include listing the property on popular rental websites, hosting open houses, and utilizing social media and other marketing channels.

Building a Real Estate Investment Portfolio

Building a real estate investment portfolio is a long-term strategy for growing wealth and achieving financial stability. A well-diversified real estate portfolio can provide a stable source of passive income, and can also offer potential tax benefits and the opportunity for long-term appreciation. Here are some steps to building a real estate investment portfolio:

Determine your investment goals: The first step in building a real estate investment portfolio is to determine your investment goals. This may include generating passive income, achieving long-term appreciation, or both.

Conduct market research: Conducting market research is an important step in building a real estate investment portfolio. This may include researching local real estate markets, identifying desirable neighborhoods, and analyzing economic trends.

Acquire properties: Once you have determined your investment goals and conducted market research, you can begin acquiring properties. This may include purchasing rental properties, investing in real estate investment trusts (REITs), or participating in a real estate crowdfunding platform.

Manage your portfolio: Managing your real estate investment portfolio is a crucial step in achieving your investment goals. This may include overseeing property management, keeping track of expenses and revenue, and making strategic investments to diversify your portfolio.

Monitor performance: Regularly monitoring the performance of your real estate investment portfolio is essential to ensure that you are on track to achieve your investment goals. This may include tracking rental income, monitoring property values, and reviewing your portfolio on a regular basis.

By following these steps, you can build a well-diversified real estate investment portfolio that can help you achieve your financial goals. However, real estate investing can be complex, and it is important to seek the advice of a financial professional before making any investment decisions.

Finding and Analyzing New Investment Opportunities

Finding and analyzing new investment opportunities is a critical aspect of real estate investing. Here are some steps to help you find and analyze new investment opportunities:

Stay informed: Stay informed about the real estate market and keep up-to-date with current events and trends that may impact the market. This can include reading real estate news and blogs, attending real estate events, and joining real estate investment clubs.

Network: Network with other real estate investors, agents, and industry professionals to learn about new investment opportunities. Attend real estate investment events, join online forums, and attend local real estate investment clubs.

Analyze properties: Once you have identified a potential investment opportunity, analyze the property to determine its potential for investment. This may include evaluating the property's condition, location, rental income, and future potential for appreciation.

Evaluate financials: Evaluate the financials of the property, including rent roll, operating expenses, and potential cash flow. Use this information to determine the property's potential return on investment (ROI).

Consider market trends: Consider market trends, including supply and demand for rental properties, economic conditions, and demographic trends that may impact the property's rental income and future potential for appreciation.

Seek professional advice: Seek the advice of a real estates professional, such as a real estate agent or financial advisor, to help you evaluate investment opportunities and make informed investment decisions.

By following these steps, you can find and analyze new investment opportunities and make informed investment decisions. However, real estate investing can be complex, and it is important to carefully consider all factors before making any investment decisions.

Diversifying Your Portfolio

Diversifying your real estate investment portfolio is a key strategy for reducing risk and maximizing returns. Here are some tips for diversifying your portfolio:

Invest in different types of properties: Consider investing in a variety of property types, including residential, commercial, and industrial properties. This can help to reduce risk by spreading your investment across different markets and property types.

Invest in different geographic locations: Consider investing in properties in different geographic locations, such as different cities or regions. This can help to reduce risk by spreading your investment across different markets and taking advantage of regional economic conditions.

Invest in different stages of the real estate cycle: Consider investing in properties at different stages of the real estate cycle, such as during a boom or a downturn. This can help to reduce risk by taking advantage of market conditions and investing in properties with different potentials for appreciation and rental income.

Diversify your investment strategies: Consider using different investment strategies, such as investing in rental properties, REITs, or real estate crowdfunding platforms. This can help to reduce risk by spreading your investment across different investment vehicles and taking advantage of different investment opportunities.

By diversifying your real estate investment portfolio, you can reduce risk and maximize returns. However, it is important to seek the advice of a financial professional before making any investment decisions.

In conclusion, "Start Small, Dream Big: A Beginner's Guide to Real Estate Investing with No Money Down" is a comprehensive guide to help beginners get started in real estate investing. By understanding the seller's motivations, making an offer, closing the deal, and managing the property, you can build a successful real estate investment portfolio. Additionally, by finding and analyzing new investment opportunities, diversifying your portfolio, and seeking professional advice, you can maximize returns and achieve your investment goals.

CHAPTER 6: CONCLUSION

Recap of Key Points

Here is a recap of key points covered in the guide "Start Small, Dream Big: A Beginner's Guide to Real Estate Investing with No Money Down":

Why Real Estate Investing: Real estate investing can provide passive income, appreciation, tax benefits, and the ability to leverage other people's money to build wealth.

The Benefits of Starting Small and Dreaming Big: Starting small and dreaming big allows you to learn the ropes of real estate investing and build your investment portfolio over time.

Understanding the Seller's Motivations: Understanding the seller's motivations can help you make more informed investment decisions and negotiate better deals.

Making an Offer: Making an offer involves evaluating the property, negotiating with the seller, and submitting a written offer.

Closing the Deal: Closing the deal involves finalizing the purchase, transferring ownership, and paying closing costs.

Property Management: Property management involves collecting rent, maintaining the property, and finding and retaining tenants.

Improving the Property for Increased Income: Improving the property can increase rental income, increase the property's value, and improve the quality of life for tenants.

Finding and Analyzing New Investment Opportunities: Finding and analyzing new investment opportunities involves staying informed, networking, evaluating the property and financials, considering market trends, and seeking professional advice.

Diversifying Your Portfolio: Diversifying your portfolio involves investing in different types of properties, geographic locations, stages of the real estate cycle, and investment strategies.

By following these key points, you can build a successful real estate investment portfolio and achieve your investment goals.

Moving Forward with Your Real Estate Investing Journey

Moving forward with your real estate investing journey involves taking action and staying committed to your goals. Here are some tips to help you succeed:

Educate yourself: Read books, attend seminars, and seek the advice of professionals to gain a deeper understanding of real estate investing.

Start small: Start by investing in one or two properties, and then gradually build your portfolio over time.

Network with other investors: Join real estate clubs, attend networking events, and connect with other real estate investors to learn from their experiences and make new connections.

Seek professional advice: Consult with a real estate attorney, accountant, or financial advisor to ensure that you are making informed investment decisions.

Stay informed: Stay up to date with market trends, economic conditions, and changes in real estate laws to make more informed investment decisions.

Diversify your portfolio: Diversify your portfolio by investing in different types of properties, geographic locations, stages of the real estate cycle, and investment strategies.

Have patience: Real estate investing can be a long-term strategy, so be patient and stay committed to your goals.

Celebrate your successes: Celebrate your successes along the way, and use them as motivation to continue pursuing your investment goals.

By taking these steps and staying committed to your real estate investing journey, you can build a successful portfolio and achieve your investment goals.

Additional Resources for Further Study

Here are some additional resources for further study on real estate investing:

Books: "The Millionaire Real Estate Investor" by Gary Keller, "The Book on Rental Property Investing" by Brandon Turner, and "How to Buy Your First Deal with No Money Down" by Brandon Turner are a few popular books on real estate investing.

Online courses: Websites like Udemy and Coursera offer online courses on real estate investing that cover various aspects of the industry.

Real estate investment websites: Websites like BiggerPockets, Real Estate Investing Mastery, and RealtyMogul offer a wealth of information and resources for real estate investors.

Real estate investment clubs: Real estate investment clubs are local groups of real estate investors who come together to network, learn from each other, and find investment opportunities.

Real estate seminars and conferences: Attending real estate seminars and conferences can be a great way to meet other investors, learn from industry experts, and stay up to date on the latest trends and strategies.

By taking advantage of these resources, you can continue your education and stay informed on the latest trends and strategies in real estate investing.